PLANETS

URANUS

ABDO
Publishing Company

A Buddy Book by Fran Howard

VISIT US AT

www.abdopublishing.com

Published by ABDO Publishing Company, 8000 West 78th Street, Edina, Minnesota 55439.

Printed in the United States.

Editor: Sarah Tieck
Contributing Editor: Michael P. Goecke
Graphic Design: Maria Hosley
Cover Image: Photos.com
Interior Images: Design Pics (page 9); NASA: Jet Propulsion Laboratory (page 6–7, 17, 23, 26, 28), Kennedy Space Center (page 24, 25), Marshall Space Flight Center (page 13), Space Telescope Science Institute (page 23, 27); Photodisc (page 11); Photos.com (page 21).

Library of Congress Cataloging-in-Publication Data

Howard, Fran, 1953-
  Uranus / Fran Howard.
    p. cm. -- (The planets)
  Includes index.
  ISBN 978-1-59928-829-1
  1. Uranus (Planet)--Juvenile literature. I. Title.

  QB681.H69 2008
  523.47--dc22

                              2007014760

Table Of Contents

The Planet Uranus

Uranus is a planet. A planet is a large body in space.

Planets travel around stars. The path a planet travels is its orbit. When the planet circles a star, it is orbiting the star.

The sun is a star. Uranus orbits the sun. The sun's gravity holds Uranus in place as it circles.

Uranus orbits the sun in about 84 Earth years. That means one year on Uranus is more than 80 times as long as a year on Earth!

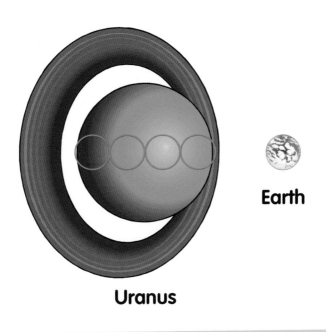

Uranus

Earth

Uranus is four Earths wide.

Our Solar System

OUTER PLANETS
Neptune
Uranus
Saturn
Jupiter

Uranus's Orbit

Uranus is one of eight planets that orbit our sun. The planets orbiting the sun make up our solar system.

The other planets in our solar system are Mercury, Venus, Earth, Mars, Jupiter, Saturn, and Neptune. Uranus is almost 2 billion miles (3 billion km) from the sun. It is the seventh-closest planet to the sun.

SUN

Mars

Earth

Venus

Mercury

INNER PLANETS

Long Seasons

Like Earth, Uranus has four seasons. But, seasons on Uranus last about 20 Earth years.

Temperatures do not differ much from season to season. This is because Uranus is so far from the sun.

Like Earth, Uranus has four seasons. Unlike Earth, Uranus's seasons do not have very different temperatures.

Summer

Autumn

Spring

Winter

A Closer Look

Uranus is the third-largest planet in our solar system. Jupiter is the largest. And, Saturn is the second largest.

Clouds cover Uranus. The clouds lie under a layer of **methane** gas. This gives Uranus its blue-green color.

From outer space, it is possible to see Uranus's blue-green color and its many moons.

Two groups of rings orbit Uranus. The rings are made of rocks and dust. The inside group has 11 rings. There are two rings in the outside group. The largest ring is nearly twice as far from the planet as the inside rings.

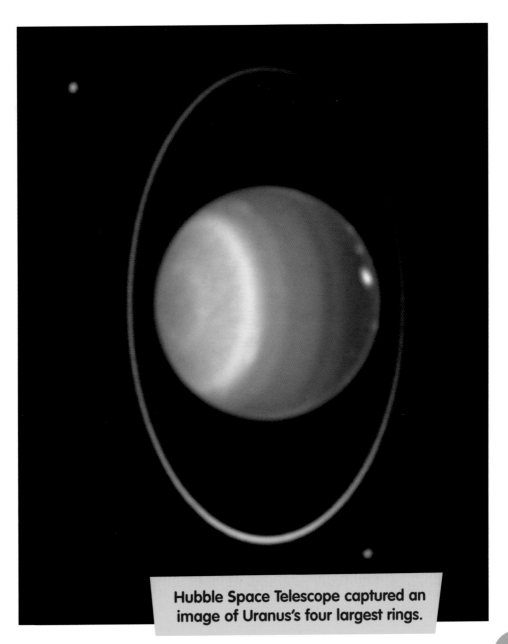

Hubble Space Telescope captured an image of Uranus's four largest rings.

13

What Is It Like There?

Layers of gases surround each planet. This layer of gases is the planet's **atmosphere**. The atmosphere on Uranus has large amounts of hydrogen gas. There are also helium and **methane** gases.

A planet spins on an **axis**. This spinning creates night and day. Uranus makes one complete spin in about 17 hours and 14 minutes.

Unlike other planets in our solar system, Uranus spins on its side. Scientists think the planet tipped over when another planet-sized object hit it.

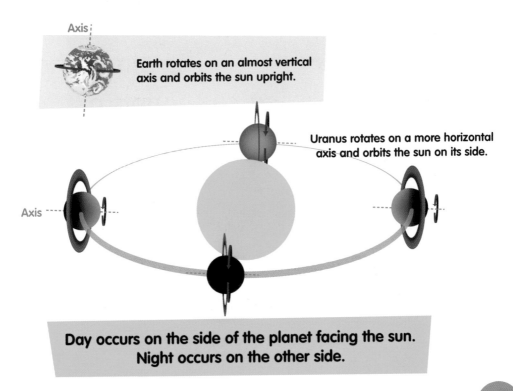

Axis

Earth rotates on an almost vertical axis and orbits the sun upright.

Uranus rotates on a more horizontal axis and orbits the sun on its side.

Axis

Day occurs on the side of the planet facing the sun.
Night occurs on the other side.

Uranus has some of the brightest clouds in our solar system. But, these are not storm clouds. Uranus has fewer storms than any other gas giant.

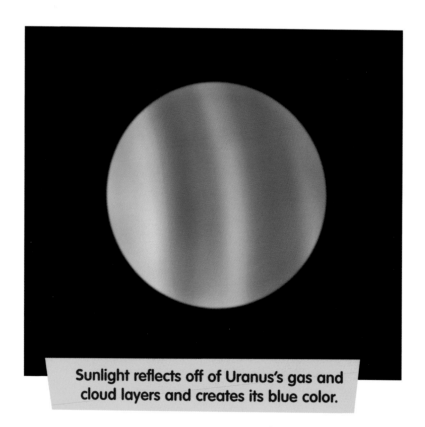

Sunlight reflects off of Uranus's gas and cloud layers and creates its blue color.

Uranus has 27 known moons in its orbit. The biggest are Titania and Oberon. Both are nearly 1,000 miles (1,600 km) across.

One of the oddest moons is Miranda. Miranda's surface is all jumbled. Scientists think Miranda shattered and reformed. This may be why its surface appears jumbled.

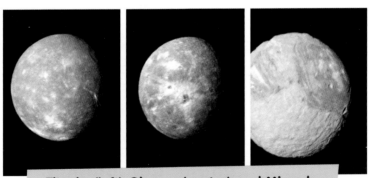

Titania *(left)*, Oberon *(center)*, and Miranda *(right)* are three of Uranus's known moons.

A Gas Giant

Scientists think Uranus may have a core made mostly of rock and ice. But, it does not have a surface to stand on. Outside the core is a layer of icy water, ammonia, and **methane** gas. Beyond this are hydrogen, helium, and methane gases.

Uranus is a gas giant. Gas giants are mostly made of gas. Jupiter, Saturn, and Neptune are also gas giants.

Unlike the other gas giants, Uranus does not produce a lot of heat. It produces only about as much heat as it receives from the sun.

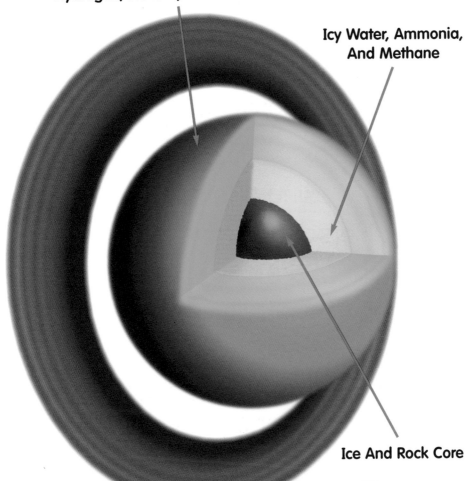

Hydrogen, Helium, And Methane Gases

Icy Water, Ammonia, And Methane

Ice And Rock Core

Gas giants have layers, even though they do not have surfaces to stand on.

Discovering Uranus

Uranus was the first planet to be discovered using a telescope. Sir William Herschel discovered Uranus on March 13, 1781. He saw a bright space object with a long tail. So at first, he thought Uranus was a comet.

Uranus is named after the Greek god of heaven. But, it took years for scientists to agree on a name for the planet.

Astronomer William Herschel built large telescopes. These helped him see Uranus.

Herschel first called it the Georgian Planet. Later, scientists wanted to name the planet Herschel or Minerva. But, other scientists were calling the planet Uranus. Finally, an editor decided to call it Uranus and that name stuck.

In 1977, James L. Elliot confirmed that Uranus has rings. He used an airborne telescope called the Kuiper Airborne Observatory.

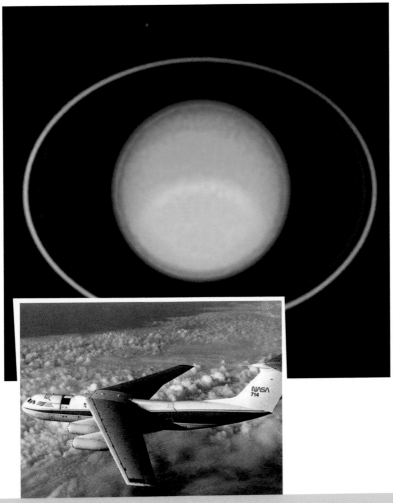

The Kuiper Airborne Observatory is an airplane that has a special telescope in it. While flying in it, scientists can gather information about other planets.

Missions To Uranus

Voyager 2 is the only **spacecraft** to visit Uranus. That was in 1986.

Scientists learned many new facts about Uranus from *Voyager 2*. Before this **mission**, scientists were not even sure how long a day lasted on this faraway planet!

Voyager 2 proved that a day on Uranus lasts 17 hours and 14 minutes.

After launching, *Voyager 2* visited four planets and their moons.

25

Voyager 2 was an unmanned spacecraft. That means no people were on board during this mission.

The *Voyager 2* **mission** to Uranus taught scientists more about Uranus's moons. This mission also showed that Uranus's rings are made mostly of rocks. During its visit, *Voyager 2 also* discovered new moons and a ring.

The Hubble Space Telescope launched in 1990. It discovered two more rings.

The Hubble Space Telescope is expected to orbit
Earth until 2013. It has captured images of Earth
and space objects, such as Uranus's rings.

Fact Trek

From Earth, you can see Uranus through a telescope.

Not sure how to say it? Uranus is pronounced "YUR-uh-nuhs."

Scientists think Uranus might have incomplete rings called arcs.

The symbol for Uranus is a mix of the symbols for the sun and Mars.

Many of Uranus's moons are named after characters in William Shakespeare plays.

Portia

• Cordelia

Titania

• Oberon

Miranda

Ophelia

• Cressida

Juliet

Desdemona

Cupid

Voyage To Tomorrow

People are continuing to explore space. They want to learn more about Uranus.

The Hubble Space Telescope discovered Uranus's two outer rings in 2005. But, the last **spacecraft** visited the planet in 1986.

Scientists still have many questions about Uranus. A new space **mission** or better telescopes are needed to answer them.

Important Words

atmosphere   the layer of gases that surrounds a planet.

axis   an imaginary line through a planet. Planets spin around this line.

gravity   the force that draws things toward a planet and prevents them from floating away. Stars use this force to keep planets in their orbit.

methane   an odorless, colorless gas that burns easily. Sometimes it is used for fuel.

mission   the sending of spacecraft to perform specific jobs.

spacecraft   a vehicle that travels in space.

Web Sites

To learn more about **Uranus**, visit ABDO Publishing Company on the World Wide Web. Web sites about **Uranus** are featured on our Book Links page. These links are routinely monitored and updated to provide the most current information available.

www.abdopublishing.com

INDEX